Copyright © 2021 by McCeil Johnson

All rights reserved. This book or any portion thereof may not be reproduced or used in any manner whatsoever without the express written permission of the publisher except for the use of brief quotations in a book review.

Limits of Liability and Disclaimer of Warranty

The author and publisher shall not be liable for your misuse of this material. This book is strictly for informational purposes. The purpose of this book is to educate and entertain. The author and publisher do not guarantee anyone following these techniques, suggestions, tips, ideas, or strategies will become successful. The author and publisher shall have neither liability nor responsibility to anyone with respect to any loss or damage caused, or alleged to be caused, directly or indirectly by the information contained in this book. Views expressed in this publication do not necessarily reflect the views of the publisher.

Printed in the United States of America
Keen Vision Publishing, LLC
www.publishwithKVP.com
ISBN: 978-1-955316-29-3

A Story About Change

Illustrated by Tuly

*For my husband, "J," and my mother, Carolyn.
Thank you for your never-ending support and
encouragement.*

Meet Kitty.

She may look like a regular house pet, but Kitty is *no ordinary kitty*.

Kitty lives with a girl named, Jennifer. A little while ago, Jennifer adopted Kitty from an Animal Rescue Shelter. Kitty and Jennifer found each other when they needed each other the most. Despite what she had gone through, Kitty was always happy. This rubbed off on Jennifer, and she hasn't stopped smiling since Kitty came into her world.

You see, I told you. Kitty is *no ordinary kitty*.

Kitty loved doing life with Jennifer. She didn't realize she was a cat until she met a group of cats. Kitty looked at the cats and thought, *"Wow, they look like me! And, what is that sound they are making? I think I can do that too!"*

Kitty meowed every day after meeting those other cats. Jennifer loved hearing Kitty *meow*.

Before adopting Kitty, people told her all sorts of things about cats. Based on what people told her, Jennifer prepared herself for life with a cat.

One day, it dawned on Jennifer that most things people said about cats were not true about Kitty.

"Cats don't like water," they told Jennifer.

However, Kitty loved water! She especially loved to drink water from the sink. Kitty enjoyed taking a sip of water from everywhere...*except her cat bowl, that is.*

"Cats don't like taking baths." People warned Jennifer.

However, Kitty could not wait for bath time with Jennifer! She would splish and splash in her small tub until all the bubbles went away. Jennifer loved watching Kitty chase the bubbles.

People told Jennifer, "You should get a dog! Cats don't like to cuddle."

Well, they apparently had never met a kitty like Kitty. She loved to snuggle up with Jennifer, especially on chilly days. Sometimes, Kitty even fell asleep in Jennifer's arms.

Everyone told Jennifer, "You can't train cats! They have a mind of their own!"

Boy, were they ever wrong. Kitty is a smart kitty, but she is also very obedient. She doesn't like to be away from Jennifer; however, she always plays quietly in her room until Jennifer is done with her tasks.

Jennifer quickly learned that you can't always *take other's word for it* — there are some experiences in life you should have for yourself. People will give you their experience, and that's nice. But who's to say your experience won't be different?

One day, Kitty had an appointment with her veterinarian. Kitty enjoyed riding in the car with Jennifer, taking in the scenery as they whizzed down the highway.

Kitty excitement was short-lived this day, because the vet didn't have very exciting news to share.

The vet said, "Jennifer, Kitty is a senior cat. Make sure you give her more time to rest and slow down on daily activity with her. She is getting older, so Kitty must be very careful, eat more nutrient-rich foods, and watch her weight."

Kitty didn't feel old. She felt young and full of energy. Jennifer didn't think Kitty was an old cat either. They went to the pet park after the visit to the vet. As they were playing, Jennifer had an epiphany.

"Your age doesn't define you, Kitty!" She said. "You're as young as you feel." Kitty smiled and continued to play and run around the park.

Jennifer wondered how much happier the world would be if people didn't stop enjoying laughter, fun, and life just because they had reached a certain age.

As they were enjoying a cozy evening together, Jennifer told Kitty some really big news! You see, Jennifer had been dating a guy named Jay. They fell in love and decided to get married.

Jennifer told Kitty that they would be moving soon. She couldn't wait for Kitty to meet Jay.

Kitty was happy for Jennifer, but she was very nervous about moving and meeting Jennifer's guy. She was afraid of what the change could mean for her and Jennifer. *Would Jennifer still hang out with her? Is Jay nice? What would their new home be like? Would there be fun pet parks in the neighborhood?*

Many questions ran through Kitty's mind.

When they moved, and Kitty finally met Jay, her fear turned into excitement. Jay was really nice, and he loved animals. Kitty really liked their new home.

She was so excited that she did not allow her fear to make her close-minded about the change in her life. Kitty also learned that sometimes, being nervous and being excited can feel the same. It is very important to learn the difference between those two emotions in order to grow and experience new things.

Kitty's new room was in the basement of their new home. Kitty loved the basement because there were so many things she could jump on. She liked spending time with Jay and Jennifer, but she didn't mind being in the basement alone. There was always a new adventure for Kitty to embark upon in the basement.

On laundry days, Kitty was excited to have Jennifer in the basement with her. She would watch as Jennifer loaded the washer and the dryer. Jennifer and Kitty would play as the clothes spun around and around.

Kitty especially loved sitting on top of the warm clothes after Jennifer took them out of the dryer and folded them.

This may sound strange, but Kitty enjoyed running up the side of doors and perching way up at the top. Why am I telling you this? Well, it will make sense in just a bit.

One day, Jennifer and Kitty headed out for a morning jog, but Jennifer forgot her keys. She turned to get them, leaving the front door slightly open. Behind her, Jennifer heard a scurrying sound and thought it was Kitty running up the door again.

When she turned around, it wasn't Kitty perched on top of the door. It was a SQUIRREL!

Jennifer screamed, grabbed Kitty, and ran up the stairs. Jennifer realized that she left the door open, and ran downstairs to close it.

Jennifer wondered if The Squirrel left the house, but she couldn't be too sure. So, Jennifer and Kitty searched the house.

In the basement, Jennifer saw a bushy tail moving near the dryer. She knew it was their new friend, screamed, grabbed Kitty and ran upstairs again.

When Jay arrived home from work, Jennifer told him about their new friend. He thought it was funny. He didn't think The Squirrel was still in the house. Jay searched the basement and didn't see anything. However, Jennifer was convinced The Squirrel was still there.

They hired a professional to set up a safe trap for The Squirrel in the basement.

Until The Squirrel was returned to his natural habitat, Kitty stayed in the guest room. She loved it there, but she couldn't wait to get back to her space in the basement.

Jay was a little different from Jennifer and Kitty. He loved woodland animals. He always fed the squirrels in the front yard popcorn.

He also loved watching the animals play every morning as he drank his coffee on the porch before work.

The idea of a squirrel being in the house didn't bother him too much. However, if one was there, he couldn't wait for it to go back outside so Jennifer and Kitty could be comfortable again.

You can definitely say Jennifer had "squirrel" on the brain. That night, she had a dream about The Squirrel.

In the dream, she was at home alone while Jay was at work. When she came into the living room, The Squirrel was perched near the open window.

"Don't run!" The Dream Squirrel told Jennifer. "I'm just here for the popcorn Jay feeds us!"

When Jennifer woke up the next day, she told Jay and Kitty about her dream. Jay just laughed. "Well, I have good news! The trapper is here to check the basement for The Squirrel again."

To Jay's surprise (and Jennifer & Kitty's delight), the trapper found The Squirrel.

Kitty and Jennifer were so happy to see The Squirrel leave the house and go back to his natural habitat.

"That's odd," Jay said "That squirrel is grey. The squirrels in our community are usually brown."

Jennifer, Jay, and Kitty chuckled. The Squirrel had given them quite the adventure on their new journey together. They knew they would always think about that moment and laugh.

The moral of the story is that change is a part of life. Sometimes, life is filled with unexpected moments and experiences. If we learn how to pivot and make adjustments, we can turn moments of discomfort to memories and lessons that will last us a lifetime.

Here's a little wisdom to take with you on your journey.

Jennifer and Kitty didn't know what to expect in their new neighborhood, or their new life with Jay. Instead of allowing an unexpected circumstance to make them run away, they adjusted. Soon, the problem went away, and they were left with memories and lessons for the next phase of their lives.

Some experiences happen to prepare us for the next chapter of our lives. An open mind and a positive attitude will ensure you learn what you need to learn to be ready for the next chapter in your life!

And always remember, whether you are a brown squirrel or a grey squirrel, a cat, or a bird, you have a place in this world. You can make a difference, but you must start by embracing the difference in yourself and those around you!

This project is dedicated to my amazing mother, Dr. Carolyn D. King Cannon. As a child, my mother read many wonderful books to my siblings (Kelli and William) and me. Her diligence in exposing me to stories at a young age inspired me to write this book.

The Izaiah College Fund

Izaiah is my amazing nephew, a bright young man with a bright future. The book you are holding is a purchase with a purpose! Proceeds from this book will go towards my nephew's college tuition, books, and boarding. Thanks in advance for your contribution.

CONNECT WITH THE AUTHOR

McCeil Johnson is a woman for all seasons. McCeil's core competencies reflect an amalgam of domain expertise acquired through 20 years of professional experience working in the areas of legal affairs and compliance. She enjoys the acquisition of new knowledge and experiences and absolutely loves helping others level up, achieve their full potential and ascend to new professional heights. In her free time, McCeil loves reading, spending time with family and friends and traveling. McCeil is available for consulting, executive coaching, conflicts management, diversity training, team development and/or motivational speaking engagements.

Thank you for reading, *Kitty and The Squirrel!* McCeil looks forward to connecting with you. Here are a few ways you can connect and stay updated on new releases, speaking engagements, and more.

LINKEDIN	McCeil Johnson
WEBSITE	www.mcceiljohnson.com

www.ingramcontent.com/pod-product-compliance
Lightning Source LLC
Chambersburg PA
CBHW041915230426
43673CB00016B/413